Brinsford books

F
GL

ERN

F

D0635333

Acknowledgements

Cover design: Oliver Heath, Rafters Design

Photographs © Aston Martin, Ford Motor Company and Wieck Photo DataBase Inc.

Copyright © Axis Education 2005

First published in Great Britain by Axis Education Ltd

ISBN 1-84618-012-0

Axis Education
PO Box 459
Shrewsbury
SY4 4WZ

Email: enquiries@axiseducation.co.uk

www.axiseducation.co.uk

This is an Aston Martin.

It is a sports car.

It is made in the UK.

It is a car that dreams are made of.

The Aston Martin DB9 Volante.

The DB9 is a new Aston Martin.

It is a new design.

It is built at the factory in Gaydon in Warwickshire.

The other Aston Martin factory is at Newport Pagnell in

Buckinghamshire.

The DB9 is a new design.

The DB9 is beautiful inside.

It is made of wood and aluminium.

The seats are leather.

This car is luxurious.

Once inside, you don't want to get out.

The DB9 has leather seats.

The DB9 is very fast.

It goes from 0 to 62 miles per hour in just

4.9 seconds.

This is the same as 0 to 100 kilometres per hour.

Its top speed is 186 miles per hour.

This is equal to 299 kilometres per hour.

The DB9's top speed is 186 miles per hour.
This is equal to 299 kilometres per hour.

It can go from 0 to 62 miles per hour in 4.9 seconds.
This is equal to 0 to 100 kilometres per hour.

It drives round bends like a dream.

You have full control.

The engine sounds awesome.

This car is glamorous.

The DB9 is a glamorous car.

This is the V8 Vantage.

It can go from 0 to 62mph (0 to 100kmh)
in 5 seconds.

It is an elegant car.

It is a car with style.

The Vantage can go from 0 to 62mph (0 to 100kmh) in 5 seconds.

Like all Aston Martins, the V8 Vantage is hand-crafted with care.

You sink into the leather seats.

The control panel is crafted from modern aluminium.

The V8 Vantage has a high-tech interior that is simply stunning.

The Vantage's stunning interior.

Here is Pierce Brosnan as James Bond with the
V12 Vanquish.
He drove it in 'Die Another Day'.
It is a very famous Aston Martin.

Only 300 Vanquish models are made each year.
It is an exclusive car.

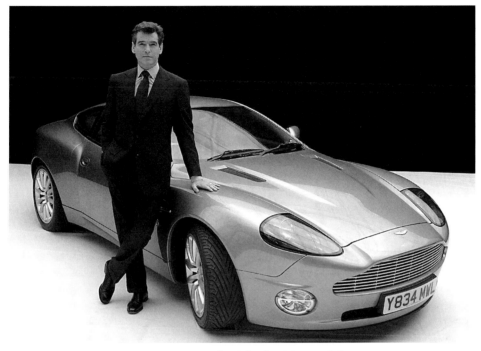

Pierce Brosnan as James Bond with the Vanquish.

James Bond has driven Aston Martins for years.
This is the DB5. The DB5 was the first Aston to be seen
in a James Bond film. It starred in 'Goldfinger' in 1963.
'Goldfinger' was the third James Bond film.

Sean Connery as James Bond with the DB5.

The DB5 is now a classic car.

It is a symbol of the Aston Martin name.

A collector would pay a lot of money for one.

However, it would have no ejector seat!

You don't get an ejector seat with the real thing!

The Vanquish S is one of the latest Aston Martin cars.

It is the fastest Aston Martin ever made.

It can go up to 200 miles per hour.

This is equal to 322 kilometres per hour.

Imagine going that fast!

The Vanquish S.

The body is made of aluminium.

Each panel is hand-built.

You can see how much care has gone into its gorgeous shape.

Aston Martin cares about the look of its cars.

The designs are up there with other high-performance car makes. Even better – it's British.

The Vanquish S has a gorgeous shape.

The Vanquish S is very powerful.

It can hold 80 litres of fuel.

It can go from 0 to 62mph (0 to 100kmh)

in 4.8 seconds.

The Vanquish S can go from 0 to 62mph (0 to 100kmh) in 4.8 seconds.

The DB4GT Zagato was made in 1960.

Only 19 were made.

Its top speed was 153.5mph (247kmh).

That was awesome in 1960.

Only 19 DB4GT Zagatos were made.

Zagato is the name of an Italian designer.

He designed Aston Martins in the 1960s.

He worked with Aston Martin again recently.

The DB7 Zagato came out in 2003.

It is a limited edition – only 99 were made.

The DB7 Zagato is a limited edition.

You can tell that this is a Zagato design.

It has a curvy design.

It has the same long bonnet.

It has the same short tail and front grille as the DB4 Zagato.

The mix of Italian flair and Aston Martin pedigree makes the DB7 Zagato very special.

The DB7 Zagato on the road.

The wheels are 'Zagato-style'.

It has a 'double-bubble' roof.

The Zagato badge is on the side.

This is a modern Zagato with shades of the past.

The DB7 Zagato.

Aston Martin has built cars for over 90 years.

It has also built racing cars.

This is a DBR1 from 1959.

The DBR1 won many races in the 1950s.

It won six World Championship races

It was a great race car.

A DBR1 from 1959.

This is the DBR9. It is Aston Martin's newest race car.
It is based on the DB9 road car.
The body is light so it can go fast on the race track.
Its top speed is over 215 mph.

Only 32 DBR9s will ever be made.

The brand new DBR9.

The DB2 came out in 1950.

Some people think it was the most beautiful

English sports car of that time.

It was even more beautiful than a Ferrari.

The Aston Martin DB2.

The DB2 was fast for its time.

It could go from 0 to 62mph (0 to 100kmh)
in 11.2 seconds.
Only 400 were made.

Only 400 DB2s were made.

Aston Martin is proud of its history.

It has a strong reputation.

It has built some amazing cars.

Buying an Aston Martin is a dream come true.

To drive one is a thrill.

Aston Martins will be special for many years to come.

There have been many great designs.

Each one is unique. Each one is high-performance.

Each one is quality.

James Bond's Vanquish from 'Die Another Day'.

Technical specification – DB9 Volante

Make	Aston Martin
Model	DB9 Volante
Engine size	5935cc
Top speed	186mph (300kph)
Acceleration	0–62mph (0–100kmh) in 4.7 seconds
Fuel tank capacity	197 litres
Price	Coupe £107,000 Convertible £111,000
Weight	1710kg
Transmission	6-speed manual or fully automatic gearbox
Wheelbase	2740mm
Tyres	235/40 ZR19 front 275/35 ZR19 rear

Glossary

acceleration	how fast a car speeds up
aluminium	a very light metal, silver in colour
automatic gearbox	gears that change as the car picks up speed
awesome	amazing
badge	the car maker's logo
cc	a measure of engine capacity
classic car	a car that is timeless, lasting
convertible	a car whose roof can be put down
coupe	a name for a 4-seater, 2-door sports car
design	the plan of how a car looks or works
ejector seat	the seat in James Bond's car that rockets him up in the air in an emergency
exclusive	special, one of a kind
glamorous	elegant, good-looking
gorgeous	lovely, beautiful
grille	the framework on the front of the car that lets air in and out
hand-built	made by hand
high-performance	powerful, fast, sporty
history	past
interior	inside of a car

kg (kilogram)	a measure of weight (just over 2 pounds)
km (kilometre)	a measure of distance (just over half a mile)
kmh	kilometres per hour
limited edition	a car model of which only a small number are made
litre	a measure of liquid (just under 2 pints)
make	the name of the car maker
manual gearbox	gears that you change yourself
mm (millimetre)	a small measure of length: 10mm = 1 cm (centimetre)
mph	miles per hour
pedigree	good breeding
per	for every
plush	smart, luxurious
quality	of high value, good standard
rear	the back of a car
recently	of late, lately
reputation	how people think of something or someone
symbol	a sign of something
thrill	buzz, joy, kick, pleasure, excitement
transmission	another word for gearbox
unique	on its own, the only one of its kind
wheelbase	the distance between the front and rear wheels